Compass and Clock

Compass
& Clock

poems

David Sanders

Swallow Press / Ohio University Press
Athens, Ohio

Swallow Press
An imprint of Ohio University Press, Athens, Ohio 45701
ohioswallow.com

Printed in the United States of America
Swallow Press / Ohio University Press books are printed on
acid-free paper ⊗ ™

26 25 24 23 22 21 20 19 18 17 16   5 4 3 2 1

Library of Congress Cataloging-in-Publication Data
Names: Sanders, David, 1955 March 4–
Title: Compass and clock : poems / David Sanders.
Description: Athens, Ohio : Swallow Press, 2016.
Identifiers: LCCN 2015044707| ISBN 9780804011709 (paperback) | ISBN
9780804040709 (pdf)
Subjects: | BISAC: POETRY / General.
Classification: LCC PS3619.A5263 A6 2016 | DDC 811/.6—dc23
LC record available at http://lccn.loc.gov/2015044707

Acknowledgments

Some of these poems first appeared in the following journals: *New Orleans Review, Christian Science Monitor, Poetry East, Staten Island Review, Mankato Review, Stand Magazine, West Branch, Zone 5, Hiram Poetry Review, New Letters, Notre Dame Review, Atlanta Review, Hudson Review, Southern Review, New Compass, Cincinnati Poetry Review, New Criterion, Other Voices, Boston Review,* and *Unsplendid.* Others first appeared in the following limited editions: *Time in Transit* (The Literary House Press) and *Nearer to Town* (R. L. Barth).

Contents

One

Pianos	3
The Mummy's Curse	4
Contrivance	7
John Porter Produce	8
Dressing the Pheasant	10
The Alternates	11
Lake Effect	13
The Observatory	14
Picture Window	16
Night Falls	19
Last Respects	20
The Forlorn Compressor	21
River Where the Lovers Wait	22
Day Trip	23

Two

Binoculars	27
Some Color	28

He Was Once 31

Box Kites at Nags Head 32

Patina 33

White Dogwoods 35

Housekeeping 36

The Skate 37

Letters 39

The Glass Branch 40

Waste of Time (The Landfill) 41

The Age of Discovery 43

Here, Now 46

Amish 47

The Seabird Diorama:
 Natural History at Balboa Park 49

Three

Dick's Island 53

The Fossil-Finder 55

Portage 57

Gossip 58

Short Wave: 1982 59

Dream of the Coal Holds 61

Mayflies 63

Unattended Consequences 64

After the Move 66

Ice Floes 67

The Lake 68

Lascaux 70

A Wash 71

One

Pianos

I saw them as a child,
in the houses of people my parents knew,
each one sulking in a darkened room
beneath arrangements of family portraits.

There I'd lift the lip
that pouted over chipped and yellowed teeth
and slightly press the lowest key
enough so that the bass note hummed through me.

I never heard the hours
of tortured practice or those mornings when
dusting hands stopped to tour again
the foreign shore of a half-remembered strain.

So much that wasn't played,
the silence resonating like the dusk
that ushers out the fall, and yet
the portraits in their frames have multiplied.

Furniture now of friends,
undisturbed and undisturbing, the strings
ease further out of tune against
the padded hammers waiting to be sprung.

The Mummy's Curse

"We'd settled in to watch *The Mummy's Curse*,"
the pastor at my father's funeral
informed us, speaking of his Dublin youth
and to our fear of everlasting life.
A silent film projector that his uncle
owned was set up in the front hall parlor
where everyone could see. They drew the shade,
a makeshift screen, which blocked the city lights,
and waited to be scared. When soon, undead,
somnambulant, the mummy left its tomb,
trailing its banners of embalmer's gauze,
the room filled with expected gasps and shrieks.
"But then we heard these otherworldly moans,
and more with every step the monster took.
The moans grew loud—a chorus from beyond."

They pushed the bravest of them out the door
and there he saw, like frozen carollers,
some passersby who, mesmerized in fright
by what they witnessed played out on the shade,
shared in the fear of those who watched indoors:
all scared of what was on the other side.
"But that was death made animate," he said,
"and rightly feared, not any kind of life."
That was in Florida, my father's final home.
The pastelled friends, whom he had hardly known,
had come to pay respects. The following day,
we took him north, to where we used to live.

Once, since then, I had some business there
and made a side trip back to tend the grave.

Recent rains had soaked our family plot,
a low spot in the village cemetery
where the marker sat, a small boat moored
amid a large and motionless flotilla.
But there would be no rising from the dead.
I thought of what the pastor had implied,
and what my brother, later, graveside, said,
whispering, "Everyone we knew is here."
To prove him wrong, I shook the spring chill off
and stuck a flower in the muck before
I drove away to look for those I knew
had staked their claims not far from here and where
I'd seen them last, when we were all still young
and on the cusp of things not named or known.
The maple-lined road I'd driven countless times
strobed in flickering bands of sun and shadows;
familiar houses shrank behind additions.
I had my bearings then that day but no
directions, and I wound up out of town
at an orchard farm I'd known of as a boy
to see if they might have the lost addresses
of those who in my mind were so nearby.
The woman working the syrup and cider shop
looked up and asked me how I was. "I'm fine,"
I said. "We haven't seen you in a while,"
she grinned, telling me her maiden name.
And then I understood the sculptors' claim
of finding the shape within the stone, and saw
the girl I'd known twenty-five years before.
We talked a while about our lives, our jobs,
before she told me where I had to go.

But even now I can't get past the fact
she recognized without a moment's thought
my face unseen by her since I'd left school.

I, who traveled far afield, put streets
between us, languages and lives and years,
returned to her and to the rest, no doubt,
untouched by time. The change was theirs, it seemed,
incremental as an orchard's growth,
but real. And I, like the unlucky dead,
would gladly move among them as their own.

Contrivance

National Arboretum

Consider these trees,
stationed on their slatted stands,
tended centuries

and trained to be small.
Root-pruned and limb-wired—such
techniques could enthrall

the quietest mind.
Appetite renders distant
the spruce one might find

clinging to a cliff
or maples burnished by wind,
positing *as if*

on each. As small as
they are, the feigned perspectives
offer up solace

(What could they be there?
What do we want them to be?
—Islands built on air!)

among their trunks, burled
and dwarfed and stripped of their bark,
in our full-scale world.

John Porter Produce

This is the shower
that every day settles the dust.
In less than an hour
it's passed. Then, a crust
of mud coats everything.

Since now it's raining,
duck inside. And though the rain won't stop,
it turns into a mercurial drop
in a bucket. Near the grapes,
a cat naps.

On the wall, a calendar
noting the days the lunar phases appear
is open to June
of last year.
Not that time stopped then,

or slowed, it's just that it has gone
as quietly as their game of dominoes,
which anyone might lose.
Eggs and fruit are what the days produce.
Each old man knows

the weight and cost of all
the goods by holding them in hand. Still, the one
who's just played his turn
weighs them on the scale
for a stranger who happened in

while the fruit sat ripening.
Step outside—
the rain has quit and the mud has nearly dried.
The sun is out
and the air, unlike before, is not so dirty.

Inside the bag, the fruit
is fresh, almost bitter, and gritty.

Dressing the Pheasant

After the knife hit the craw
of the bird gone stiff and cool
with ice and time in transit,
I removed the seeds, still whole,

from below the cocked head
and fingered them like beads,
one prayer apiece, as if grain
picked from the gullet of a bird

were of greater grace than if not,
in a hunter's boot, let's say,
shook out and left to grow,
or before the bird was shot,

if hours had passed and the seeds
had broken down and turned
into the spectrum of feathers
that rose out of its nest of weeds . . .

But when all the seeds that filled
that sack inside the bird—
the rest of the broken string—
slipped out and spilled,

I could not make them more
than they were:
undigested and wet on a paper
bought for the occasion, the chore.

The Alternates

for Margaret Neill

Faced with going home again,
where you grew up and all of that,
you take the normal route, a road
connecting town with county, one
in which a set of simple turns
turns down your own gravel drive.
They don't occur to you—the alternate
ways you'd sometimes walk—pastures,
farmers' woods, really not much
more than seasonal display.
But at the time they drove you down
into their thick. You came out
the other side, nearer to town,
replaced by someone who saw more
than you had seen going in:
yourself, of course, a half an hour,
an hour, older.
                    They seemed amused,
the few villagers you saw,
when they said, as in my case,
"David, what brings you to town?"
Remember how you walked among them
as if with news they'd not yet learned?
Maybe they'd known all along,
patient while your knowledge, light
at first, grew large—a weight you wore,
ill-fitting and obvious.

There were times you felt you'd grown
to fit into it. You had not.

Years after you had moved away
and tried to map the fading routes
back home, they were, from any number
of directions, always paved.
The others had not disappeared,
still there, somewhere, thickening.
They just would not occur to you.

Lake Effect

Look at the childless couple
watch from their window upstairs
as the moon turns the snow

into another source of light.
They point to the tracks they've made
drifted but unfilled

like a string of bells sunk upside down
leading to their door,
and they pretend to wonder

what lumbering, starving beast
has disappeared across the lawn,
down the walk, retreating

into the past or more likely
into the snow falling by now
in the next county. They catch

in the window their own faces
lit by the moon. Her husband whispers,
"Tomorrow morning, early,

before the snow melts away,
let's follow the steps of the beast."
His wife squints her eyes and nods.

"Come down, now!" you ought to tell them,
although their rooms are silent with dreams
and already filled with the light of day.

The Observatory

The oddity's how benign it always was,
the building with the slotted silver dome:
a giant screw, sunk into the ground.
Do the kids next door ignore it? The curved brick front
is nearly blocked from view by evergreens.
Do they know or care about what goes on
when the stars come out and the campus traffic dies?
The roof slides open on the night sky.
The swiveling dome loosens and tightens, by turns,
the hold it has on its groomed plot of earth.

Once, a kid next door myself, I heard
the drone of mowing in the distance and found
the front door propped ajar. I knew whoever
had left the place unlocked would be a while.
I slipped inside, adrenalin on cue.
Past vacant offices, desk and books
in sight, I stepped into the circular room
and waited for my eyes to find the dark.
Amid the cranks and rails, levers and wheels,
the one great window shut like an eye midwink,
the telescope poised, I guessed, at a purposeful angle,
I wanted the natural secrets to fall away
right there, illumination even in dimness
as when the building comes awake at night
and the giant eye slowly opens again
ready to study the tunneling reaches of space.
I considered my ignorant awe a thing to be rid of.

Instead, the gears and scaffolds, the flawless lenses,
the barrel aimed at the retractable roof gathered

in quiet against me. What did I expect?
What answers did I not have questions for?
I knew less then than when I'd entered. It was,
after all, day. Mostly what I knew
and felt was small, as in YOU ARE HERE
way left of center in the Milky Way,
not merely in this place where in the maps
and charts of night surely something happens.
Worldly then, I backed out slowly, unsteady
in the rush of sun, taking nothing away.

Picture Window

*I was the shadow of the waxwing slain
By the false azure in the windowpane.*
　　　—Vladimir Nabokov

From the chair in the room
in the house on the hill
she sees the world (a world)
in the ripple of hills
where the road slips by
and all becomes green again
until night, which is black
but flecked with farm lights,
and, if it's clear,
the red, green, and blue
lights of the airport
that let the viewer know
where the horizon is.
It's this she searched
with her field glasses,
the school bus stops,
the ambulance racing
through the hills,
someone crossing the meadow,
a tractor's progress
in a field above a woods
above the top of a barn
and silo, looking, looking,
the lenses' resolution failing
under the weight of the distance.

But in her own backyard,
which seeps away to field,

she keeps close track
of the birds that flit
from the top of the trees
to the brush by the spring
that comes out in the rocks
that the farmer who lived nearby
(when this was all farm),
in order to clear the land,
pushed to a low place
he used as a dump
where now can be found
his dishes in shards and tonic
bottles cracked open,
mud filled but still corked.
The birds splash in the water
and cover the mud
with hundreds of barbed-wire tracks.
She doesn't see those,
just the focused mesh
of branches and birds
flattened in magnification,
starlings, forsythia, red-winged blackbirds.

It's the smaller birds,
wrens and sparrows,
that on occasion,
when she's in the kitchen
or some other part of the house,
fly over the yard
and into the window
as if into nothing
and shake it like the punch
of a fist. She comes running
often to nothing
if the bird was just stunned

and has flown away, but
sometimes in combing
the grass below the window
she notices a bird lying dead.

For if something were standing
in the sunlight
outside in the yard
or flying toward the window,
what it would see would be itself
among the trees and grasses
but not the woman or the room.

Night Falls

Dover, New Hampshire

Where the lucent underwater knives
of lights reflected from the bridge
pin back the river's weave
like black bunting, it arrives

at the rim in time to fall
in one long silver sheet
that never stops. The continuity,
the gravity of it all.

The falls at night
is all I want to remember here:
the river's lulling, if endless, explosion
turning the boulders below to a kind of light.

Last Respects

Every day I walk to lunch and pass
a rectory and church, and that's okay.
The pigeons clap their origamic wings
and lift off from their perch. The stained glass
barely lets the light inside a way
past the window: a cold glow there. Such things
don't bother me at all. Yet when I meet
a crowd of old folks gathered in the street—

one of their number gone—I stop but try
not to watch their time of personal
grief. And if it's dulled, displayed so often,
I'm sure for them to know that when they die
whoever's left will throw a curse on all
that darkness with a simple stifled cough in
a hanky from a midrow, hardwood pew
is some assurance. And if the hearty few

who come are fewer than the time before,
I guess this is as good as they can do.
There must be comfort just in giving up
those precious mornings to the oaken door
that only opens outward. I watch as two
pass by to greet a third who's living up
to expectations and beyond. They bend
and start to weed the walkway with their friend.

The Forlorn Compressor

Not exactly sad—
how could it be? (impersonal,
hidden, mechanical)—
but definitely rude

kicking itself on
somewhere across the valley
at all hours of the day
and night, and just at dawn . . .

No, rather a reminder
of all that I'm unsure of,
like love and the resonance of love.
I'm tired of the dynamo's candor

that fills the valley when it kicks off,
when the silence abounds,
lacquering the charitable sounds
of traffic, the insects' persistent laugh.

River Where the Lovers Wait

Bats come here at dusk to hunt,
following the insects' paths that loop
above the water. From the shore,
I toss a handful of stones in the air
and watch the bats dive then veer
from that wrong, unfamiliar pattern:
they, in their way, know better.

Day Trip

We walk through dreams like this:
accepting, unsurprised, a little
distracted, as if nothing were amiss.

Last spring the river rose
and left its flotsam lodged in trees
like squirrels' nests. Who knows

what forgotten betrayal or regret
it would, if this were dream
and not reality, represent?

And when the river shoots canoes
downstream, past us,
who, wading out, nearly lose

our footing, what lost passages
might those be? Who knows or wants to?
And what guarded messages

didn't I find in the luna moth,
its celadon wings intact though frayed,
lying on the hard dirt path

back to the cabin? I wanted none.
This is no brilliant, double world
of dreams, only the semblance of one.

And if we run into a squall
on our drive back home, let's
let it mean little, or nothing at all.

Two

Binoculars

A gull barks from a fishing boat
and the waters fan out
as the tide comes in
like radio waves are said to fan.

The mansion across the cove
is up for sale, so
says a waterfront sign.
Behind the gull's chuckling
a radio plays
country pop; the song carries,
though it's tinny and low.

The landscape crew
has broken for lunch under the pines,
thinned and pruned to allow a view—
from the windows of cool and otherwise empty rooms—
of white masts, shrunken to unlit wicks
in the stiffening light.

But where are the owners
who have packed up their things?
Have they packed away their dreams as well?
Or are those included in the asking price,
invisible to even the aided eye
somewhere the other side of the cove?

Some Color

It's snowing this afternoon and there are no flowers.
                —Donald Justice

i.

The world at large would have us believe the truth
can take us just so far. And where we will
our minds to play those daily tricks on us,
those trompe-l'oeil and -l'oreille, it's there that life
would be unsettlingly bright and misted and cool.

Late autumn morning along the river road,
a scenic highway slightly too far off,
the mist keeps veering toward the brink of rain.
With each weak squeal of a broken accordion,
the wipers smear the windshield, blur the view,
then clear it, briefly, before the rivulets
gradually obscure it again.
                                    The road shines black
like the varnished bark of the trees whose limbs
lurch over the swollen stream and over
the ragged enclave buried along its banks—
a bevy of old vacation travel trailers,
aerodynamic if stationary, aqua
fishing cottage, and squat, red-trimmed cabin,
all flanked by Bondoed pickup trucks abandoned
as if in some urgent need to fish—
a caravan that never broke camp. In the weeds,
children appear and disappear like game
protected in a wildlife preserve.
A fire smolders in an oil drum.

At this sullen onslaught we check the signposts
to reconfirm we're on the right state route
to take us south to where it meets the Ohio
at its western turn. The maps do not show
Old World remnants sprung from intermittent
sunlight and economies of need,
sodden with exclusionary charm.
They cling to us like ticks along the way.

ii.

Does the new truth wedged into the world,
the arrangements made you're most happy with,
become your life when grafted on the old?
What once surprised me now is more a puzzle:
idly searching the web, I type the names
that I wrote last on classroom valentines.
None comes up most times or none unique.
For the few, like yours, that do—and here's what's strange—
they've disallowed the raw yet stable data,
not just glossed over lost and fallow years,
but forged another place or date of birth,
switched a sibling's gender or adopted
a mother's maiden name.
                                    Identities
recast—what padlocks do they pick open,
what terraced rooftops do they look out over?
The same storm front and distant hairpin turns
that dullards deem mere unleavened facts?
They must be fresher views, if lonelier,
with the many ways you've learned to say good-bye,
the salmon dusks achieved with sleight of hand . . .

iii.

Soon, in late winter, some miles south of here,
near the banks of the Ohio River
the planting begins. Annuals from seed
sprout, take root against their better nature.
Imagine the beds bathed in the glow of glass,
long factories of light and forced warm air . . .

Impatiens, dianthus, salvia, think how
they're loaded into flatbed trucks on pallets
in early spring and sold in flats for cheap
at farmers' markets, home and garden centers,
and nurseries for their one quick season.
Once they're out at the cul-de-sacs, on lawns,
or massed under saplings that buttress municipal buildings,
and set in the dirt, treat them lovingly,
as if they could have been here all along
and belong here, as they do now, being
what and where they are so well: some color
introduced into the indigenous green.

He Was Once

Affected by the weather and amazed
by simple things, for instance, the slight stain
of his own shadow that the moonlight spilt
on lawns long after everyone was sleeping.

So when he drove the widow to the top
of the mountain to watch the incoming storm
with him, she was taken aback somewhat
when he compared himself to the quiet air,

calling it *yellow, volatile but unshaken.*
Beyond the pass, they saw as they sat there
the clouds amassing. And she asked, as from another
life, as he sat gazing out, to be taken home.

Box Kites at Nags Head

Cape Hatteras, early 'sixties

Every year, my brothers built a kite:
wood, paper, glue, and string.
Every year the try at flight
was a nervous, tenuous thing.

Before it finally put out to sea
they tied it to a log.
A bottled note, of sorts, part tree,
part architectural flag.

Merchant vessels crawled the horizon,
and fighter jets would buzz
the waves, in training for some good reason
(those years, there seemed there was).

But no deliberate plane or boat
ever concerned the summer craft
of log and kite kept afloat,
aloft, by what they couldn't lift.

Patina

The bell above the restaurant door rang madly
when a group of noisy breakfasters
filed in, but we kept to ourselves.
We were, I thought, complete. As bronze corrodes
to green, left to the elements, we in our own
slow way had somehow turned.

                                But the scene ignored us:
checkered cloth, bits of egg and jam
on heavy plates, the coffee. We watched the faces,
safe, distant, all sit down and then
returned to our discussion—what was it now?
—my father's fine gestures, her mother's strained
embrace. The waitress served the group their food.
We straightened up the morning paper and left.
Outside, quiet—only the weeds' whispering,
chattering as steadily as radio static.
It's not enough to know I should have guessed
or seen the shadows under conversation
pulling the silence tight against our words.
Our bellies full, we were still months away
from never looking back. And even then
as I pulled open the door to the car and watched
this panel of world swing by in a flash, there,
in the car window—restaurant and weeds, the sun,
and us—as if gravity'd released me
and I saw the earth in its spin for just an instant,
I recalled what she who sat in the driver's seat
checking her hair in the rearview mirror told me
after one hushed stretch of Arkansas road: she said,
"Once I saw a bowl of fruit—bananas,

apples, pears, and oranges—amazing colors—
polished to a waxy gloss. Finding
they were made of plastic did not diminish
my delight. I wasn't sorry or
insulted that they had given me that much.
Do not be sorry or insulted now."

White Dogwoods

The season of buds broken into bloom
we watch progress is a slow surprise.
And yet we start when, there behind

the other trees complete in their green
experiment, the white dogwoods
seem to be those patches of sky

that break behind a stand of trees
edged up ahead by a field or valley
as one approaches the end of a woods.

And though this may be a blurred reverie,
it's hard to consider them a promise
of more than beauty, a preparation

for the usual greenery. We give way
to our constant waning attention
after the papery ornaments have fallen,

a flurry in the warm breezes,
and we avert our eyes from the trees
now simply green, to the white on the ground.

Housekeeping

The living pack us up.
Now that we have gone and died
it's comforting to them
to know what's left is tucked inside

a box, an urn, or closet
where memories, like dreams, abound.
They tend to the mess
our dying first has left around.

(Letters dried to mica,
clothes gone further out of style,
souvenirs of us
in storage, kept a little while.)

They allow themselves sadness,
drifting near this windy border.
But grief has raked out its embers,
which cool and die among the order.

The Skate

for WCB

I.

You must know the myth how woodblock prints
of the floating world from far beyond
the curly-headed winds came to the West
as packing stuff for porcelain. That's how
cautiously I carried the cartilage
off the sun-stenched beach, bleached eye-sockets
like scissor finger-holes, mysterious keel.
Beneath the nylon kites skimming the cliffs,
beneath the boy's small feet skirting the surf
to chase the toy blue football, it washed ashore
worn in the foam by each succeeding wave,
of interest only to scavenging sanderlings.

II.

I once saw horses hurtling over the sand,
somewhere the other side of this body of water—
France, Nantes, I think,—outside a casino,
lifting themselves off all four legs, buckled
in the unsupported transit Muybridge made
famous. Again, I was an alien—
an urchin, slow and spiny. Mawkish as
that sounds, the slowly colonizing world
beyond the rubberized seaweed's beachhead assault
had its unfinished business too: lotions,
fish-painted pails, coolers, glasses, sandals,
terrycloth cover-ups, towels, canvas bags,

boogie boards, paperbacks, boom boxes,
small talk, and boiled lobsters, these
demanded my attention be secured,
a rented respite from the constant scrubbing
that peeled the flesh from the tender lies, for which
this served a temporary carapace.
My lie, I confess, is imbuing myself
with needles and crunchy exoskeleton, safe
in a tidal pool far from the water's reach.

III.

The skate arose unmindful of itself
and unsupported in its undulations,
no bone at all but for this whittled bit
of buoyancy, all else cape and current,
a carpet unrolling along the ocean floor,
luxuriating in the mottled rays
of light and darkness.
                                  Once ensconced in luggage,
the ivory shiv passed through security
and entered my inland home where I unwrapped it
and rinsed it off in scalding water. And there
it bent and broke. Resistant to my pinch,
a pliable piece of plastic until it wasn't,
now never to call to mind my find nor turn
to sand. Unfortunate, that. Unlike me—
leaving a summer mirage for somewhere else
(no place the shore anticipates the tide)—
awake and lucid, nearly in control,
if you could call it anything like fortune.

Letters

There is a boy who brings your groceries.
It is a late afternoon in November
or a little after lunch in the spring.
Either your friend will meet him at the door
or you yourself will sign the bill
and give him a tip. And he will not think
he will remember as he walks down the stairs.

And maybe now you are dead and he is grown
and feels old as he crosses the Charles River
between work and home. There, perhaps,
you will catch him look past his grocery bag
at you licking the glue on an envelope to be mailed,
closing it firmly between your fingers and thumbs.

The Glass Branch

They say when lightning strikes the shore, the path
it takes is like a quick nerve burrowing
beneath the beach. And in the aftermath

of fused sand, a branch of glass. A little
like thought made deed, the blast of energy
cools off in formation and turns brittle,

grounded in its own design. The storms subside.
Whether it stays buried or is exposed
and shattered will be determined by the tide.

Waste of Time (The Landfill)

You can never see it,
even from the top,
only the access road
that opens itself up

like a pulleyed curtain
at the picture show.
Still we throw things out.
Where will they go?

Over the angry side
of the sheer ravine.
You can't see it,
but it's been seen:

what was specific—
animal, vegetable, mineral—
has merged over time
and is now very general.

The rinds of breakfast,
their teethmarks lost,
mix with the unstuffed chair,
cat-scratched, tossed:

all have their stories,
the stored-up hours.
How many, do you suppose?
Look, now ours

are being flattened,
pushed around, made
into another mountain,
even as they're unmade.

Imagine working here!
A man sat on the rim
of the canyon in his truck.
In the seat next to him

a baby, a dog, or his lunch—
I couldn't tell which—"Where
should our things go?" He pointed
to a spot as close as we'd dare

get to the edge, where we let
loose the untolled measures
of time, in the shadow
of buzzards, and time's erasures.

The Age of Discovery

It's lucky the boy was strong enough
to lift the top of the hardwood box,
which was as long as he was tall.

He raised the lid to grab the doll,
the doll that was once his mother's
when she was a girl, a favorite toy,

a baby doll (there were no others),
stored in the box, swaddled
in newspaper, brittle and yellowed,

over the many years and moves
it had weathered. Unsteady
in his hands, its long gray gown

covered its limp gray body
of padded cloth, the plaster head
gone bald with age, its eyes closed.

The lashes lay against its cheeks
like iron filings, if filings could
be tamed to lie in even rows and curl.

When he sat her up (she was a girl),
in the crook of his arm
her eyes sprang open to reveal

a sparkling blue, which, not
quite human, looked real
enough set in balls of alabaster.

He cradled her head and rolled
the eyes shut, then open again,
a natural, familiar gesture.

And when he went to lay her down
the back of her head barely struck
the edge of the box and the plaster ·

broke as neatly as the shells
of eggs his mother cooks
for his breakfast Sunday mornings.

He heard the furnace roar
to life like the ocean, and the concrete floor
beneath his feet began to sway.

He felt his throat closing tight,
but as he looked around the basement,
the washer and dryer stood still and white,

the deep freezer hummed as it always did,
and the light streamed in the window
on the open box and doll,

and he could see inside her head
the counterweight of lead
swinging the eyelids open and closed,

as he rocked her up and down.
He reached his finger in to operate
the weight and watched her eyes respond:

up and down, they blinked,
in gravity's plan: true plumb.
Gently replacing the sleeping doll

in its paper crèche, facing up,
along with the missing piece,
he closed the heavy lid of the box

and shut the basement door,
and shot upstairs to play outside
in his fields, and forts, and creeks.

Here, Now

A group of young punk rockers congregates
on the street, this still summer night,
looking restless and somewhat lost,
toying with their locks and ideas of lust;
as if nonchalance were a studied move,
they don't approve of me or disapprove,
and not a parent, I likewise am not blessed
with the baggage that accompanies the child.

Instead I watch them, knowing how I cursed
the Ohio sky that kept me from the wild,
and how we made it seem like somewhere else
with all that one garage band could call forth,
without imagining it would come to this,
for all that it was and wasn't worth.

Amish

I still see him
walking his bicycle
out of time
on the tertiary dirt road

and up ahead,
freed of the daytime cringe
of electric fences, the herd
he worked slowly toward

the barn. Like slack reins
slung with gravity,
one-strand phone lines
led them uphill.

This was not his farm.
And in the cut crop field
a combine lay
quiet, its giant yield

having earned its keep.
Other hands had gone to town,
each in the market
for a woman to winter on.

And while I waited idly
in my father's Thunderbird,
down the road the car's
stormy rumble was heard

but ignored. I saw
from the back the cross
of suspenders and, when he turned,
the naked face,

which signifies a single man.

The Seabird Diorama
Natural History at Balboa Park

Captured,
they froze,
suspending
animation—an act
denatured,
which lacked
a proper ending,
not this pose:

the mother
never quite
reaching the beak
of the other,
her chick,
stuck in an infinite
yawn;
and us, looking on.

Three

Dick's Island

So this is your lot.
After the years you've spent
filling your house
with items discarded or bought
at ridiculously low prices,
knowing someday
someone would walk in willing to pay
more than you,
plain and simple,
the fire marshal or whomever the island's citizenry
appointed to such duties as this
has declared your house
unfit for public perusal.
And your response,
to your neighbors' horror,
was to move everything outside,
right in front of the main thoroughfare
in full view of passing tourists.
We've bicycled the circumference
of this entire island
as tourists are wont to do
and you haven't moved an inch
unless it was to turn the page of your newspaper
(not today's, by the way)
and yet when we stop to talk,
your generosity is as suited
to this island as the round smooth stones
washed ashore and by chance of nature
balanced one atop the other.

You start telling us of your miraculous finds,
croaking in a way that suggests
you haven't spoken much today
or yesterday, except to ineffectively scold the kittens
who wander away from their own pile
of newspapers like loose and furry
tentacles over the rubble. Their thin high voices
nearly opposite from yours,
lost in the whitecaps' crash
against the narrow beach, mostly pebbles.
We've come here to get away
and see the monarchs' migration,
but you stay here year 'round,
even when provisions come in just once a week,
and the jagged ice spreads out from the island
like a cape of iron slag.
—Most like an island then, I suspect.
Even now, high above the tallest trees
in twos and threes, the deliberate
orange butterflies, all compass and clock,
rest and gather and move on, away from here.
And we, straddling for balance, go right on cycling.

The Fossil-Finder

Leaving the house far behind,
while his friends, two lovers, quarreled,
he studied the ground at his feet to find
a proffered world.
Where a stream had worn a limestone trough
he washed off
a rock he had unearthed,
then dried it on his pants.
It was etched with prehistoric plants
whose stems looked like the broken legs of birds
set in stone. He wanted to see if
when he showed his friends
they would notice that, though of no real consequence
lying there in bas-relief,
these living things had turned to rock
long before their own centuries of human talk.

At the screen door he stopped,
hearing just the distant cough of thunder.
They had done all talking
they were going to do. The house was quiet.
But whether in a fit of love or in a fight,
he'd have to wonder,
not going in but walking
toward the car. A lesson
now without a reason
might as well remain unlearned. There he dropped
the fossil in the grass,
content to wait out the coming shower
and reconciliation and where, before the storm would pass,

he knew (a man with too few words),
the rain on the car's canvas roof would shudder
like the pecking of a hundred birds.

Portage

Those mornings before the sun
had burned off the fog,
when she looked from her room
over the roofs and trees
and white steeple receding
in the thin curtains, she liked to imagine
an ocean there, out past the point
completely obscured by the fog,
where one was said to have been,
long ago. And once
considering the false proximity
and having dismissed it as that,
she fell quiet and heard the wind
sound through the leaves
like the dull shatter of waves
breaking somewhere beyond
the strict white steeple,
enough to make her look again
and want the fog to stay.

Gossip

These days the chatter turns to friends
who've quit responding to our letters,
a brave but botched attempt at love,
the neighborhood: bulletins that, for us,
preëmpt the evening news.

And though all the time we chide
ourselves for passing on what we've heard
(prolonging rumors by our whispers,
sad facts not even we should know and yet
make sure the others do),

it seems that this is flesh and muscle
and so makes somewhat tolerable
the bones and joints that prop us up:
cold houses we walk into afternoons,
the bulk mail, the bills.

Short Wave: 1982

for John Burrow

Long after the lovers have had
their fill of radio requests
and turned toward simpler, unsad
hearts humming in their nests,

and I myself have nodded off
sometime before my oldies show
ended with "Goodnight, My Love,"
as it did last week and two weeks ago,

you're at home with astral voices—
broadcasts of a different band—
pulling in the global noises
that somehow likewise pull you in.

Leaning forward in your rocker,
to ease the tuning dial,
gently, like a safecracker,
until the tumblers finally fall,

you've tuned in to what you want to hear:
idling cars and satellites,
the whole cacophonous atmosphere
sounding like a summer night's

Babel—tappings, flutters, a shrill,
full, makeshift orchestration.
In among the high-pitched trill
you move on to a steady station,

a program in a foreign tongue
bringing the Voice of America and a
serious provincial song
to you (a subtle propaganda

providing a touch of history
like an out-of-town but major paper).
Who else listens to our coded mystery,
the atonal music of at least one sphere?

Some god who's more than what he does
but cursed and sickened by what he hears?
For him, silence is a far-off buzz.
For you, the air is dark but clear.

Dream of the Coal Holds

Past the stand of pines
that barely hides a family plot
where all the stones but one
bear the same last date,

and the slat-gapped barn
perched in its defying tilt,
which, year by year,
becomes more unbuilt,

then right at what's left
of a farmhouse (one supposes)
beached like the ribs of a ship
on a reef of wild roses,

railroad tracks emerge,
a half-mile down,
weed-strewn and unused.
Followed around

the eastern bend they come
on a building made of brick,
squat and off to one side,
the top even with the track:

a series of chambers, really,
connected by doorless door-
ways, each room with a chute
down which they used to pour

the coal. I stood there once,
my camera in hand,
with the ghosts of my grandfathers
over from England—

coal men, *collyers*
they were called. I did not
see them standing there
till finally I brought

the camera to my eye
and focused the lens
on the repeating frames
and empty holds. Like friends

at a rare reunion
they smiled shyly or scowled
for the fraction of a second
the camera allowed.

And it didn't seem strange or wrong
to have seen them suddenly there
only odd that I'd carried them—
unknowingly—that far.

Mayflies

The way the pond popped you'd have guessed
a light rain had broken out—not fish.
Hatching mayflies hugged the surface, a frail mist
that shook the water alive. Their one wish
(if you could call it that)
was to mate
before they died. It had taken years
to come this far.

Years later
what I remember
is not what was said
that quick weekend, or our cottage bed,
but the whiskered tails
and opal wings like shattered glass,
and the morning after, with its thousands of small bodies
scattered across the grass.

Unattended Consequences

Root-rutted and boulder-blocked, the road
we took was more a riverbed than road.
Long since behind us, the towns and shopping malls,
the sterile starter mansions, farms, the mobile
homes in stages of impermanence
the mortgaged rich could never comprehend.
Once further in, we hit a logging trail,
or remnants of one. The sun flashed through the leaves
like fish brought up in nets around us. Saplings
whipped the truck and left my arm in welts.

Pointing up ahead, my neighbor asked,
"See that maze of flowers? See the outlines
that they make? A row of houses, right?"
As dutiful as ramparts at a ruin
the flowers lined the walkways that weren't there
and stitched themselves across the ghosts of porches
before unraveling throughout the weeds.
"Timbermen—who knows when or why—
tried to settle here, built some houses,
then disappeared. Left just the daffodils . . ."

Such curiosities should be passed on
to kin, not just the guy across the street.
But anyone who knew my neighbor's brood
would be surprised if his small talk displaced
the plans for home improvement or the game
that week as grist for dinner conversation.
Their interest in his "hunting lodge," a cabin
atop a shaded riverbank, was slight

apart from its potential resale value.
In all fairness, though, he chanced to tell me
just because the daffodils were up—
their temporary heads of yellow crepe
both maverick marks and mockery of survival—
the afternoon we saw them in the woods.

We drove on to his cabin, locked down last fall
against the elements, cleaned out the leaves,
oiled hinges, swept the floor, and watched
the river for a while before returning.
As I said, he mentioned this in passing
and didn't think about it much himself.
And whether the small community collapsed
under the weight of human needs or else
went up in flames, the dazed inhabitants
clustered around their blazing fate, trampling
the plot where the daffodils had taken root,
was not among the details shared with me.

After the Move

At night on the street one car
at a time descends in the distance, like a wave
uncurling across the face of a cove,
falling to nothing on the rain-soaked tar.

I could be either wave or driver.
I know the crab paths of the way-
ward traveler: it's no harder to leave than to stay.
Behind our house is a river.

Each time the tide goes out
mud cracks and peels on the rocks.
How like, how different from a pond it looks,
that has worn the suffering of an August drought.

Ice Floes

Driving home at dusk across the bridge
I think to look upstream toward the floes,
the glossy islands anchored where they froze
cushioned by the warmer leaden water
separating them like flux and solder
in an ornamental window. Best to hedge

against that stillness. For when the traffic light
turns red and I myself come to a halt,
the scene beneath me shifts: each slab and fault
sails past, fluidly or nearly so,
and in that vertiginous minute when what I know
was moving stopped but what I thought just might

be static started up, I get the notion
that this may be what death is like—below
the textured surface a steady unseen flow
slowly working, leaving me behind—
or worse, what our lives are like, and find
a world I didn't recognize in motion.

Ease off the brake. The traffic's peristalsis
begins anew. I roll my window down
and listen to the evening carillon
of horns and rusting mufflers above the ice:
the usual fare but tonight a voice,
almost, in concert with whatever calls us.

The Lake

Emptiness is a thing man cannot bring himself to believe in:
that which is not, is untrue. That which is untrue, is not. So our
efforts to find something where we see nothing are unceasing.
—Tagore

The news is brought by a ball of birds—
a molecule gaining number knowing, somehow,
beneath the water the frightened fish
in their schools were making a mad dash
for the surface as if pursued by a whale.
But what lake has a whale? We've heard
of lakes that rumble before a storm,
the water black as the sky is black,
or calm when the sea is so.
And there is the lake in which one can throw
a piece of wood, which comes up petrified,
or rather encrusted in a case of stone.
I have a relic on my desk
from there, a serviceable paperweight.
There is even the story of the one in Coimbra
that "absorbs not only wood, but even
the lightest of bodies thrown in it,
such as cork, straws, feathers, etc.,
which sink to the bottom and are seen
no more." But this one, the one
with no whales, that the birds roil above,
its surface is breached by flotsam and jetsam
from shipwrecks that happened at sea
many miles from here, way beyond the surrounding hills,
the patchwork fields bordered by ancient hedgerows,
the small villages whose names on the map

extend like fishing piers edging the ocean.
Through subterranean passages, it is supposed,
the debris makes it way magnetized to this place. And so
like the others who stand along its pebbly shore
looking for lost luggage, heirlooms, loved ones
who wash up from untold distances and over years,
I take my place scanning the surface for those telltale puffs
as if muskets were being fired from beneath,
bagging a bobbing treasure.
Some have set nets or fishing poles,
which let them leave, to go about their lives,
and come back later at their leisure.
And even in winter I've gone down,
though my hopes have all been dimmed,
and stood examining the expansive sheath of ice
to look beneath it as a kind of game.
Only the frozen lotus pads and their ornamental pods,
not much but beautiful all the same,
and I join the bundled others, in their separateness,
field glasses strapped around their necks, staggering along
the pebbly beach, each step leaving a nest of stones.

Lascaux

Jacques Marsal, who as a boy discovered the prehistoric paintings of the Lascaux cave with three friends and became the cave's guardian for life, died Saturday after a long illness.

—(AP) July 17, 1989

The first day, his dog disappeared in the forest,
lost down a hole. The next, exploring with friends,
he found the cave—leaping stags, buffalo,
prehistoric horses.
         Alone a moment, one French boy lived
a dream boys dream: to stand at the place
where for thousands of years no one has been.

That was 1940. Boy and dog are dead.
And the moment? Well, moments are always disappearing.

after Miłosz

A Wash

This is a local scene with hills,
houses. One will see, if one looks,
how it's composed. The grasses fill
the otherwise blank space. The strokes

of bare trees cling to the landscape
in a winter without snow. Numb
blue mountains, small and distant, rip
roughly across the horizon,

and the sky, also, is a blue.
Birds, like a stream of ashes, fly
toward the granary below.
And there, in the midst of this, lies

a town, a town with a railroad,
a depot, a humming engine,
and a man standing in the cold
air, which whips him like wet linen,

removed from it all on a bridge.
Note the view. This is what he sees
and less. The slackened foliage
dripped over stones in degrees,

without severe perfume, the lack
of voices here, the long applause
of trains—he's learned above these tracks,
and what's missing is less than loss,

though also his. This is what
we can guess: he'll retie his shoe
before we leave, or maybe not. But
we know he won't move on; we do.